LITTLE ELEGIES FOR SISTER SATAN

MICHAEL PALMER

LITTLE ELEGIES FOR SISTER SATAN

A NEW DIRECTIONS BOOK

ACKNOWLEDGMENTS: Some of these poems first appeared in the following print and on-line publications: *The Best American Poetry 2019, Bomb, Brooklyn Rail, The Canary Islands, Connection* (anthology, Zasterle Press), *End of the World* (anthology, Seattle Poetics LAB), *Harper's Magazine, OEI, Posit,Seedings* "Missing (Persons)(s)" first appeared in "The Poet and The Critic, and one missing," an installation and on-line event curated by Lauren Mackler for MOCA LA. The Kafka translation on page 79 is by Michael Hofmann and the Pessoa translation on page 93 is by Margaret Jull Costa.

Manufactured in the United States of America
First published as New Directions Paperbook 1500 in 2021

Library of Congress Cataloging in Publication Data
Names: Palmer, Michael, 1943– author.
Title: Little elegies for sister Satan / Michael Palmer.
Description: New York : New Directions Books, 2021.
Identifiers: LCCN 2021001830 | ISBN 9780811230896 (paperback)
Subjects: LCGFT: Poetry.
Classification: LCC PS3566.A54 L58 2021 | DDC 811/.54—dc23
LC record available at https://lccn.loc.gov/2021001830

10 9 8 7 6 5 4 3 2 1

New Directions Books are published for James Laughlin
by New Directions Publishing Corporation
80 Eighth Avenue, New York 10011

Contents

MIDNIGHTS

LITTLE ELEGIES FOR
SISTER SATAN

First Elegy

Singing is prohibited in this café.
Torture is permitted in this café.

I'll have a double, thank you,
in ¾ time, Sister,

may I call you Sister, you
almond-eyed, unsmiling,

in this ever-changing light
that cloaks the feral world?

These dancers, do you know them?
Do they think

as they glide and spin
of what is to be

and what has been?
Do you know their names

and if so
do their names change

from earliest hours to late
and day to day?

Do their wounds show
as they mimic the music's path?

(Sister, I apologize, but I must ask.)
Hiroshima, Nagasaki, Abu Ghraib,

Oradour, Terezín, Deir Yassin,
Vel d'Hive, Vorkuta, Magadan—

that waltz, that dance—
among the café candles

and beyond the fogged windows
the endless allée

of lightning-scarred trees
whispering fractured words

for none to understand.
All the beautiful names,

Sister, the infinite names,
roll off the tongue

innumerable as the stars
that frolic in the sea.

Second Elegy

Sister, is it not time
for us to learn to speak

now that the infernal machines
have captured the breathing word?

Now that drones fill the sky
over Santiago de Chuco,

Central Park and Unter den Linden?
Is it finally too late

in this welcome winter rain
to cross the singing bridge

to that place where
memories of the future

bend like cypress limbs
under ancient snow? Where

the plague years melt away
and the shrill voices of children

explode from the mist
with nothing but pain

and praise to sing,
as if one and the same,

like two bodies joined
in a last embrace?

And these cypresses,
ministers of mourning,

how is it we applaud them
in their grace?

Third Elegy

The clock is a fiction, dear Sister,
yet we live within it,
Sister, its arms are ours,

and the fiction is as real
as a rose in the steel dust
and you will recall, dear Sister,

that each of us is the sum
of the two preceding numbers
in the talismanic series

and that this ever expanding,
radiant and more than perfect
spiral will swallow us

so said—was it Zoroaster—
from a distant cliff
his spider-arms outstretched

on the face of a death's-head clock.
And it is there
within the span of those arms

that we recall
what we were not.
We were not what we thought

to be and to become
not the architects of desire
not the thieves of fire

nor gardeners nor plumbers
nor workers in steel,
only the painted puppets

of parallel lives, only
the uninvited guests—ghosts—
at the beggars' banquet.

Elegy for whom or for what?
We watched the frothing tide
gather time in

and it meant nothing
at all to us then
or at most some spare thing

that could not be freely said,
a wound of salt-laced water
and a gasping

mouthful of sand,
while deaf to those measures
which draw us together.

Fourth Elegy

At last the perfect weather is unending
even as the ice storms prove unending
even as what was once eternal
departs like a brief smile

as we swing from life to life
like sad-eyed clowns
in whiteface and baggy pants
balancing on red balloons

between the simultaneous worlds
the parallel worlds
we have yet to name.
Sister did the Lords of War

once offer you a name?
Was it the same
one they offered me
at the point of a gun?

Did we then live on
telling unspeakable tales
over a thousand and one
unending nights?

Lift the ice and the sun
to your lips, Sister,
and to mine. And sing
the words between the lines.

Fifth Elegy

Oh, body, where are you going,
body of the earth, lost
double, lost copy of the body
mute body of yesterday
in tomorrow's shredded cloth?

Oh, body, where are you going
in the fog of the body
in the mist of thought
in the body of another
known and not?

Oh, body, have you watched
the Dioskouroi dance
as one body in two
on the quantum tips of fire
while an ensorcelled earth spins below?

How many languages, how many limbs,
are scattered along the roads
of this earth? How many sounds
meeting their anti-sounds?
How many books burning

to light the way?
How many pure believers
to shatter the icons
of the pure believers
while the ensorcelled earth spins

on a turtle's back?
Our jaws churn to emit a song
that will retune the body,
return the body, dear silent earth,
gone where?

Sixth Elegy

Here, Sister, it can be said
that good-bye means hello,
day night, far near, here
where the rivers run uphill
and the clouds lie still

and your shadow, ghost sister,
emits an incendiary light.
Sister, we have ridden the mute centaurs
and firebirds round and round in the dark
and slowly learned to spell

without words, gauge the ebbs and swells
of the untellable tale. Praise the infinite,
nameless tellers of tales
swaying from the poplar's limbs.
The wind belongs to them.

To us the breath,
the frayed thread, the turn
and return of the juggler's stolen song.
Nothing to know, nothing to tell
of the now and the then after all.

I see the world is mad, sings Kabir,
who knew neither ink nor pen
as he wandered the islands of this earth
where up is ever down
and song has no sound.

Seventh Elegy

> "Again, we are ourselves
> no more ..."
> —Nichita Stănescu

Our bodies, Sister, such
as they are, almost touch
but transparent as they are
we pass through one another
as if on the way

elsewhere, on the way as if ...
Sister, I've lost the thread
and need to begin again—
for days no words have come, none
to say *elsewhere*, none

to say *body*, none to say *begin* ...
Sister, I saw three children
hanging from a tree, their slender
bodies tilting in the breeze.
Why three?

Did poem or war or dream
place them there?
Mad poem, mad war, sober dream?
I saw a house of ink-dark glass
and Minerva's Owl flying backwards

toward that city with a future
never to be. It's there we learned
those countless lessons about falling,
night falling, and the inner sky, it
too falling, and the masters of Doo-Wop,

Techno and Ska,
of tone row and dice throw,
and the angel-winged messengers
of Utopia, their showers of light
and open-tuned guitars, the Green

Dancer in her flesh-clinging mist,
Flora and Kiki and Mme. X.,
glistening Ava, fading Echo
and, silently, the Anti-Icarus
falling among the concrete cliffs,

his welcoming arms outstretched.
City of conjurors and crumbling gates,
mute buskers and alphabets aflame—
Sister, your match perhaps
that lit the paper path of names,

list I found inside your eyelid
that one brief afternoon,
knowing no more
where we begin
or when we end.

Eighth Elegy
(los caballos en el aire)

In a digital dream
or on the silver screen
Invisible Sister said:

Whenever sperm pours from my breasts
I am forced to ask,
What sort of fountain is this?

Child of empire,
child of Sarin,
child of the atom split

that I am
split in half that I am
in a chemical dream

or on the silver screen
whenever black ink
seeps from me

I am forced to ask,
Who has been entertained
by what they have heard

and what they have seen?
Child of phosphorous
raining upon rooftops,

ancient child of the archive,
its filtered light, its
dust in which desire

surges and sleeps
and where the horses—los caballos—
of my splintered nights,

los caballos en el aire—
what need of earth—
lift slowly through the dust,

slowly rise, they
have no need of time,
they have the madness

of horses in their eyes,
they slowly rise, they
encircle, they turn

and return, they entertain
as if the music were their own.
There is no end to it.

They have the madness
of horses in their eyes,
the madness of the archive

where I reside.

Ninth Elegy

All elegy is fragment
sings the crazed sister
as she hurls
wine glasses and dinner plates
from her apartment window,
the remains of a meal
still upon them.

Her clothes follow.
Every figment is real
sings the naked sister,
the now naked sister,
contemplating the body that was,
the one that is
and the one it will become.

Afloat in the air the clothes,
and the hours soon follow,
both first and final,
until none remain,
neither minutes nor seconds
to count out loud.
And always in the air the horses,

circling, prisoners of air,
their songs heavy as air,
light as a stone of bright quartz.
They too are ensorcelled, these horses,
and she watches them slowly falling.
Falling, she watches them.
Who hears her calling?

Tenth Elegy

Sister Satan declares, Elegy is liquid no it is air.

Sister Satan declares, When poetry reinvents itself without words, I will be first in line to listen.

Declares that when sex reinvents itself without the flesh, I will be first in line to make love.

Asks SS, And were I to lower myself by taking up the pen, what then?

(For one must lower the hand to lift the pen.)

SS declares, In the lost hours of night, the truth of my thoughts comes alive, only to be extinguished before day arrives.

So an ocean of chemical waste has spread across my desk.

What to make of its beauty?

Sister Satan declares, The forged elegies are home to me. We drop them from helicopters into the sea.

Declares, I have hidden a rose upon my person or within,

and within the rose a homespun mourning cloak,

and within that cloak, no body that you know.

Sister declares, I have not spoken of my village, my underworld, the comedians and cosmologists who gathered there,

ecstatic and vacant-eyed,

to toss now worthless coins into the River of the Fathers

if that was its name

on the eighth day of each week of the thirteenth month of the year.

I loved then the names of the trees: the holly, the copper beach, pin oak and holm oak, ailanthus, chestnut, slippery elm and winged elm, red maple, chokecherry, paper birch, red alder, dogwood, stone pine, Scots pine, mountain pine ...

Though in truth, Sister Satan admits, I can name none of them with certainty when I see them.

And in truth, Sister Sadie declares, the words I am using here to speak of myself I might just as well use to speak of a tree

or of a physicist undressing time by means of light, a solemn infidel like myself,

ambling along the banks of the filthy Tiber, under a swerving cloud of starlings at dusk.

There more than once have I sung the Four Last Songs to an audience of none.

Have sung or been sung.

And if as well I celebrate too much the Devil's Trill, as some would claim, it is what rings in my aging ear,

hands, throat and tongue no longer my own.

Sister Satan further declares, That semen stain left somehow upon me lingers like the scent of hashish in a steamy room, whose space at once expands and contracts, like elegy annihilating the past,

that stain shaped like the Angel of History's isolate tear,

while kind Sasha in Petersburg slips the eye of an almond into his mouth, and sweet Elena serves us wild garlic from the mountains and passes me a forbidden cigarette with a wink,

and with any luck we confound the agents of grief.

(Rome—St. Petersburg—Rome, Nov. 2015)

Eleventh Elegy

I was blind then, then a thread, then an effigy sledding toward the sun.

Then a child falling unnoticed through space and into the sea, a painting of the sea.

The sea an abecedarium.

It did not save me.

Dear Sister, your sisterhood didn't save me, didn't ease me.

Sister, may I still whisper us out into the evening for a walk, a walk by the sea, even if we are centuries—or light-years—apart?

As we walked near the Tiber that time, laughing like fools at the ruins, clasping screen memories to our breasts, and swallowing heavy metals from the Book of Songs.

Cobalt songs, chromium songs, cadmium songs, antimony, mercury, zinc, and always just then, some listener would inevitably complain, You have gone too far, sailed too far.

And where, pray, the elegy, where the Hanged Man, the Knight of Wands, the Sun, where the downbeat and, once again, the elegy?

And where, Sister, the aged pair bent ear to ear, and where now the poem, so-called, the noetic poem, the poem of unknowing, meant to be placed here, stumbling along this path "near the Tiber," and where the words of summoning?

The sea an abecedarium, a palace of memory, declares the poem, so-called, while dealing out cards.

Hierophant, Knave of Hearts, Higgs boson, ancient cards dealing them-selves.

Sister, pardon this interlude—it came about by chance.

Today, as ever more each day, the innumerable bodies adrift in the sea—
who will count them, who claim them, these particles?

Sister, you once said, It is what it is; once said, You must change your
life; once said, Words don't mean anything; once said, You must wait.

And I waited in the alphabet's shadow, waited, in the half-light, for eyes
to turn from grey to green, for the words to reveal their names, waited
for the cicadas and the night-birds to speak.

In this world, with its two suns and two moons, perhaps desire and grief
are the same.

Who will count, who will claim?

Elegies: First Commentary

They tell me now that the dust of stars and the compounds of the flesh are essentially the same.

What if I had known this earlier in life?

When I think of "possible worlds," I think not of philosophy, but of elegy. And impossible worlds. Resistant worlds.

Among the dead, that is while walking through cemeteries, people often remark favorably ("poetically") upon the silence, the "peacefulness." On the contrary, in such places I invariably experience a cacophony of voices—unfinished conversations, viral arguments, lovers' yearnings and regrets being expressed. It is only along the traffic-lined boulevards, with their teeming sidewalks, that I hear nothing.

When, as writers, we put words in people's mouths, we hope they will one day understand.

We hope that friends betrayed, or neglected, across a lifetime of distraction, will understand.

"For all we've said in a contorted fashion, we ask forgiveness." (Yoel Hoffmann.)

These rivers and seas that seem to flow endlessly through my pages, the glacial lakes and the estuaries as well, and the lovers or former lovers somehow always near as well as far, far-away-near, speaking and silent, transfixed by one thing or another, and the pronouns cast adrift, as if in a storm (though today the skies are clear, the weather calm).

We, in our primitive state, still needing machines in order to fly and devices with which to
speak
to one another.

A young modal logician, a veritable prodigy, takes his pleasure by beating equally young women with his belt. Eventually apprehended, he claims it is necessary, "because there is no joy to be gotten from philosophy."

Many things bring me to a state of near paralysis, as when the demands of form, its counterlogical certitudes, begin to take hold, without so much as a word.

How necessary, this coming to a halt, this inaction, this interruption of what we might think of as "the flow."

Silent days, nights as well, do pass in that way, almost defiantly, from time to time.

So why, as the moments of immemory accumulate in such silence, am I thinking randomly of Aira's ghosts, of Turing's enigmas, Baalsrud's escape, the lost poet of Harar, the beaches of Agnès, Darwish's doves, his ailing heart, his ashes and dust, the carousel in winter, at rest, and of the pseudonymous Chris Marker, his quantum flights across time?

Why Chantal, last October, her final hours?

Why Celan, Collobert, Mayakovsky?

Tsvetaeva, Rosselli, Nerval?

Forrest-Thomson, Pavese, Primo Levi?

Yesenin, Trakl, Kleist?

"But tell me if you know ..."
(Dante)

Elegies: Second Commentary

Poetry was dead again
they said again. So then

I wrote about my life
as demanded, a "memoir" they call it,

loves, losses, triumphs and sorrows,
glimpses of the future-past,

the before and after,
salt-tears and laughter,

that sort of thing, though sadly,
I told it all encoded.

Elegies: Third Commentary

It is true that I write by hand
in an indecipherable script.

That is why, each day, when I return
to the illegible page

I must begin again
from the beginning, and so

the following day and the following
days with their reddening skies

and unsayable words, Sister,
unspeakable words, Sister,

and unpredictable winds,
winds as invisible as words

lapping at the slopes of Mount Analogue
where boulder and bindweed caress

and where the upward winding path
has no end, the too bright air

growing thin as we ascend,
thinking of nothing

but breath, mountain
glowing clear as glass,

we two breathing barely
before the sun's

eye of noon,
blind eye, blinding eye,

there where we were done with words
at last, by silent agreement.

And so, Sister, it is also true
that today I wrote nothing

and yesterday
same as you.

WORLD ENOUGH

Street Song
(17th & Mission)

"She is gentle when
    breastfeeding the clouds …"
        —Zbigniew Herbert

Mad Mary sits on a stoop
        She tells
how she's birthed the Christ

    many times
    sometimes in rain
    sometimes in snow

sometimes amidst the flames
    of war in the streets
I have traveled many leagues

    beneath the sea
    far so much farther
    than the eye can see

and the little I sleep I sleep
balanced on a blackened bier
swaddled by the news of the day

    from near and far away
    I carry death in my pocket
    that loving friend

    and I'll pull him out
    when the song must end
    What more is there to say

Poem Ending with Words from Mandelstam

"I have forgotten the
word I wanted to say."
—O. M. 1920

We wash our feet and enter the house of prayer
where no one is present no one absent
and where the voices of the beloved

are chanting words they do not know
and cannot hear
The leaves of autumn have gathered there

to listen and to whirl about the floor
It seems that they dance it
seems that they mourn

curled inward as they are
skin and veins grown stiff
and they rustle in the bare breeze

rustle as if to sing along
to summon the unsayable
names one by one

in the flickering half-light
amidst the sacred scents
and feverish eyes

Beyond the doors blind swallows pierce the mist
and the poem's forgotten word
waits beside a river gone dry

word that asks too little
word that asks too much
while waiting for what?

Four wheels without a cart?
An angel with no form?
A prophet with no tongue?

Transparent the names
Transparent the manes
of the horses in the dark

(for Ashraf Fayadh)

O Sister

O Sister lichen
are growing
on the once creamy thighs
of the poem

Los años the years
Homero writes
los años know
and we do not

Solunar Tables

Pain of the child set afire
before blindered eyes
a world's eyes

Poem of the bird
exploding in flight
in our random skies

Pain of the ladder
its storm-shattered steps
defying ascent

Pain of the Hunger Moon
dangling over hoar frost
by a failing thread

Should we cut it
for those without bread
Pain of the word

Poem of the word
unheard unread
The darkling river

and the steadfast ferryman
who refuses your coin
The wave that embraces

while it destroys
Our secret entertainments
at the Madman's Market

and our alphabets without end
that spell themselves
and weave themselves

into a trembling web
as the poem-road below
of silences and stones

comes to a final turn

They

They love Brecht
now that he's dead

Of many poets
this can be said

Notre Musique

I imagine the film.
It is not it is finally not

called
Notre Musique after all.

I can imagine
the film we imagined

though there's nothing
strictly speaking

that I can imagine.
That is to say

I can imagine nothing,
but nothing more,

or nothing,
but nothing else.

Once in the library
there was a fire

and the books consumed the fire
while the authors of the books

stood idly by,
the authors in eternity

among the buried words
beneath the pavement,

the authors among the flies
on a heap of dung

in a fallow field,
the authors lost at sea

in a storm of words,
the authors shorn of memory,

the authors in rags
in a film called Notre Musique,

a silent film now
playing almost playing

at the Orpheum
or is it the Thalia,

the Clio, the Melpomene
or the Music Hall of Vagrant Souls,

a nameless film of endless length
forbidden by the designated

descendants of the prophets.
Admission free.

(pour Liliane)

Clear Day

The poem
discovered an island where there was none
It watched
people roam along its shore
Some climbed
toward the crenellated walls
of the ruined fortress
from there to view invisible ships
approaching
their sails afire and full
in the late sun the poem
has long forgotten the purpose
of these walls, these rusted
cannons and their mounts,
these sails drawing near
And what of the memories
of the people themselves the poem
places here, strolling
with their children and their dogs
amid the intemperate gulls,
the pipers and sanderlings
Always the minutes pass
sometimes with no words
and the poem
is happy with this,
content with no words,
thinking of the fortress,
the blazing sails
and the violent peace
of evening as it descends,
the shimmering night-sun
of sea and page
And in the lost poem, the
poem asleep, the invisible
bodies of other, distant children
appear suddenly from the sea

scattered along the shore,
limbs already half buried in sand
by what force of storm or chance
And its eyes rolling the
poem asleep
confronts the compass rose,
calls west to east,
unseeing counts the hours,
the liquid chain of stars

(for Manuel Brito and
the 25th Anniversary of Zasterle Press)

Site Series: The Lady of Glass

First one, then another, then a third. Am I remembering right? First one, then another, a third, a fourth and then how many more? Perhaps all, engulfed, enthralled, transformed. Or maybe none, none at all.

First one, then another, a foot, a leg, a torso, an arm. The neck, the eyes, all our eyes, am I remembering right? As we turned, now one, now another, into glass. As glass replaced flesh, we became instruments of light, so it seemed, at once hard and brittle, gleaming, ready, in an instant, to chip, to crack, to shatter.

First one, then another, and a third, all unwitting, unwilling, we entered the crystal world, our limbs growing stiff, no longer obedient. We grew still.

We who had reveled in movement, in the raising of a cup, the clasping of hands, the wave of an arm, the leap, the turn, the ecstatic joining of bodies, were still.

But still? We became, after all, liquid bodies, formed of sand and samphire, heat and salts, earth, fire and water. Light continually passing through us, stillness and motion at once, hard, yet ready to crack at a sound or a blow.

One, then another and another, all taken up, infected and transformed, Markus, Jennifer, Habib, Franco, and how many more? Was I the first to be so changed? The source? The carrier? The cause? Or had it come to us all, in a fever, at once?

The process was gradual. I awoke one morning from turbulent dreams and felt a kind of languor spreading through my limbs. I gazed at the fingers of my left hand, then my right, and watched them grow diaphanous, as if melting into air. Wrists and thighs, the neck growing rigid, the face, their faces . . .

As my transformation began, I remember, I think I remember, that a glassy sea of words appeared to me: time, memory, silence; breath, sinew, storm; horizon, voice, shore; sanctity and war; space and song. More too that I can't recall, all afloat there, gently bobbing, like small ships at anchor. Stillness and motion.

What colors, what hues, did we take on? Markus became the color of the sea, Habib, young wheat, and Jennifer the luna moth she had always been. Franco, black ice; myself, how could I tell? How remember? And Megan and Margaret, the color of laughter and ash and spun glass. Was I the source, was I the cause? Could we then see through ourselves? Into ourselves? Could we even be seen? Could we speak? Words of glass, we who had sung. We who had celebrated.

Was it borne through the air or through the blood? Through words on the wind or the fevered workings of the mind? Did the thoughts of one become those of another, and another, until they were taken up, encased, emptied out?

Was I first or last, or just one among many, to be caught in that stillness, that shimmer of silence, transfixed, nothing but a lens? Would it end?

Missing (Person)(s)

I did tell you the story but you've forgotten it.

You never told me the story.

We were walking along the Tiber, speaking of its wounds.

I have never been to Rome.

You remarked on the black nail polish all the women were wearing and on the youth of the musicians on the bridges.

You never told me the story.

You had said you wanted to know, to hear it for yourself. Were I to tell you the story again, would it matter?

Should it?

It's hard to say.

What was the story about?

It was about a missing person, though actually it was about nothing.

How can there be a story about nothing?

It was just a story. It came to me as we were walking along the Bundt, after a drink at that writers' bar.

I've never been to Shanghai.

Perhaps you were missing, a missing person in Shanghai.

How is that possible?

It's possible in the story, if you think of it as the missing story.

You said it was dark, a dark story.

Maybe, maybe not—it was so long ago.

How long ago?

Weeks, years, it's difficult to say.

Tell me anyway.

All That Jazz

Got suddenly
olda, brotha,
remarked the master
tenorman to me
one late night—*it*
took me by surprise—
had to improvise.

Nord-Sud

That day when I thought of Pierre Reverdy
for the first and final time

I counted the butterflies in Rome.
In Rome I counted the butterflies.

There were always three,
three on Trajan's blood-stained column,

three within the Memoirs of Hadrian,
three alight on the Virgin's left thigh,

three perched amidst the eternal dust.
(I counted to three because I felt I must.)

Electric blue were these creatures of air
born of the mind of Pierre Reverdy

mourning the death of a violin by fire.
The Tiber is flowing somewhat lazily today

past a distant echo of Pierre Reverdy,
past the burning manuscripts of Pierre Reverdy

lighting the banks not of Tiber but of Seine.
I counted the butterflies in Paris then

as they caught fire one by one,
one by a lock at the Quai de Valmy,

one by the dying guillotine
on the Place de la Cloche Vide

where three last songs could be heard.
You waved graciously and sang along

as poetry, that ballerina in flames,
bid you farewell while taking one last bow

with no regrets other than a few.
The earth is perfectly still

and the butterflies have ended their day
in the north and in the south.

Listen, Pierre, the hands on the clock
point toward the snows of yesteryear.

Pierre, you died as we were about to meet.
This poem is to be continued indefinitely.

All

All the beautiful women in my life
were called Sadie or Sadist I forget
the color of that flower also its name
now that you ask

where I have been these past few months
between the solstice and the total eclipse
of all that we once had known
or thought mistakenly to know.

Perhaps the snow blinded us
or we gazed too long at the startled sun
forgetting our strict instructions
like so many others

who had assembled there for the event
that came and went
without a word without a breath
while the dancers so young filled the streets

and the fields with a sort of silent song
thinking they could go on and on.

(August 24, 2017)

Hotel NY

The hotel of my childhood
spoke several languages at once.

I marked the box for None of the Above
and pointed to the sign:

No Pets Allowed.
The river froze solid that winter

and the kindly whores huddled in doorways,
their litheness undiminished to my eyes.

Ice seemed more beautiful than childhood,
its enveloping silence and bluish light,

no words required,
only the premonitory

winds of change assembling
along the half-deserted avenues.

The hotel of my childhood
spoke several languages at once

in its desperate need to be loved
by its privileged guests,

its celebrants and suicides
now here now gone.

I Know a Silent Movie Star

I know a silent movie star named Jane.
She speaks without moving her lips.
She once starred in a film called Shadow Train.
Her memoir is full of lies.
She's perfectly honest about this.
Such is life as we know it
and if you don't like it just turn the page
until you arrive at the one that feels right
since you can always find another
on some distant sister world
I was told many times as a child.
I love Jane because of her silence
which I've tried unsuccessfully to emulate
throughout my adult life.
Lately it's become a bit harder for me
to walk and breathe and sleep. We all love Jane
because of her unbridgeable distance
like that far-off sister planet
on which life can barely be imagined.
She is nonetheless a star not a planet.
She retains her cool and distant glow
even as the superstorms here
grow ever more violent
and the surging tides and flames
display themselves to those many miles above
circling and dreaming their circular dreams
in endless earth orbit.
I know a silent movie star named Jane
though that of course is not her actual name
only that of the distant star
she once suddenly became.

The Cats of Cremona

When the silent symphony engulfed the city
even the naked emperor was forced to sing

When the snows of yesteryear suddenly reappeared
the poets of dust drew a deep breath

and said, Let us begin, let us begin again
not from the beginning but from the end

And when everywhere the E-strings suddenly burst
the cats of Cremona flashed a smile

that lit the deep night
so that even night's hooded guardians

retreated in fright
and the bell towers and spires trembled at the sound

and the novels of romance untold their tales
of corsets and rustling silk

and who knows what
And who knows what

When the silent symphony engulfed the city
even the solid citizens were forced to dance

twirling on their crutches as one—
undoubtedly a kind of waltz—

as the naked emperor watched from above
a stain of secret knowledge on his lips

that only the cats of Cremona could see
And in the ancient, twisting streets below

each of us recited our silent parts,
sleepers and singers both,

caught between thought and breath
as the emperor fondled our naked hearts.

The Bell
To complete the tune

the trumpeter raises the ember,
the glowing coal to his lips,
the pentacle, the pistol to his lips,
between known time and no time.

To complete the tune
after a chorus about silences and seasons,
after a chorus about hours before evening,
hours that accelerate as day wanes,
hours like pages torn from a notebook

and fluttering to the floor,
pages of new snow, snow
that like a tune is silent,
snow with a hint of blue in it
here and there like a tune ...

To complete the tune
he raises the bell of the horn,
there where he and the bell, the bell
of the horn are alone, knowing
that the music in the room

and on the stairs is not his own,
knowing that he must undo the tune,
that it must not flow,
must come out wrong,
since such is song.

(to Wadada Leo Smith)

Look

The light of dawn is before us
the blind ballerina told me
as I peeled the stain of sleep from my eyes

and after me the deluge, you will see,
said the blind ballerina in flames
spinning and spinning in place,

and all the machines, she said all
the machines of death are beautiful
as they refashion earth and sky

and forge screams out of songs.
And all, she said all
the banned books are blessed,

the burning books are blessed,
look at how they dance in the flames,
look at how they light the city square

and warm the faces assembled there,
look at how their words
ascend through the thick air.

And caught in the rising wind,
she said, look at how they spin and spin.
They could land anywhere.

To . . .

And so your final poems:
that almost wordless

triumph of nothingness
over death

At Readings

They ask me now at readings
about the strange creatures

suddenly turning up in my work—
you, Sister Satan, among others—

and I try patiently to explain
that as my truest friends in this life

begin one by one to vanish
I must find new ones, equally strange.

Thinking of Distant Wars

Thinking of distant wars
we walked along a country path
heavy with dust.

We walked and we bathed in the dust.
It slowly coated us
as we talked of distant wars.

Only so many words left, you know, she
said, only so many words left.
We've used up so many, you know.

Where'd they go, I sometimes wonder?
Where'd they all go, she asked,
shredded like old cloth perhaps,

swept off by wind or flood
or tossed onto a pyre
of what once must have been story

or once have been song,
a fire around which
good citizens gleefully

danced, excited by the light
such words cast perhaps?
Only so many, you know,

she said, for now and for then,
words for now and for again, for
when. Only so many wars left,

how many wars left, she asked,
words left, she asked,
as we walked along a twisting path

heavy with dust.
The sentinel crows watched over us,
took stock of us,

did they laugh at us,
at our ridiculous
earthbound gait

on a path dissolving beneath us,
a path of black glass—no—
a path of bruised flesh

melting beneath us?
Crow of Infinite Sorrows,
Crow of the Eighth Day,

Crow of The Other Voice,
Crow of The Art of War,
of Solitude, of Slaughter.

Only so many, she said,
only the infinite steps.
Surely you must know, Old Crow.

We passed the dreaming chimneys,
the burned stubble fields,
the herms and the scorched

and sundered alphabets.
Only so many letters left,
I thought she said

speaking as if
she were the wind itself,
the war itself, the dust.

The Poem and Its Double

never speak
to one another.

The darkness of one
is the light of the other.

The silence of one
forms the sound of the other.

The tears of one
are the unheard

laughter of the other.
The loves of one

are the lost
loves of the other,

lost words, last words
of the other.

The meanings of one
are lost upon the other,

echoed within the other,
erased by the shadow

of the other. Each lies awake
in the other's sleep

and views unimaginable scenes
through identical eyes they

do not share.
Both dread the sovereign hours

yet each listens with care
to the green

ice of time crumbling,
the sudden whir of wings passing,

the enfolding tales
of the cloud of unknowing.

(for Richard Sieburth
who knows of this)

In Any Case

A dream of Merce Cunningham at some large theater, rehearsing with his company. He tells me of a kind of entr'acte Artaud is writing for the company. I realize that had I not failed as a poet, I might have been invited to write it. In any case, we are all dead.

There

I have had poems published in countless journals over the years.

Now, I officially withdraw them.

There, that's better.

The Child Soldiers

The child soldiers arrived
and severed my tongue.

Have you not mistaken me
for someone else?

inquired the tongue
no longer my own.

Yes, perhaps we have.
Does it matter, really matter?

they asked as one.
Is it not the blade

that matters,
the keenness of its edge,

the language that it speaks,
the one that it silences

and the one that it invents.
The child soldiers arrived

as in a dream,
impossibly young,

so eager at last to please,
so eager to play and to sing.

The Palace

Somewhere there's a bank
wrapped in grey stone
that is always being robbed.

You can hear the alarm.
Somewhere there's a poem
being written in the dark.

You can hear the quill
scratching along the page.
You can hear the poem

crying out in alarm.
The poem is in chains.
It yearns to be free.

The poem
like the bank being robbed
in the lines above

has no value.
It is alarmed
by this terrible knowledge,

alarmed that it is alone
in the palace at 4 a.m.
and that dawn may well have decided

never to arrive again,
and that the lovers
have long since fled

the palace at 4 a.m.
itself built of bones
suspended in space

as its maker once proclaimed.
An alarm has sounded.
It echoes through the vaults

of the bank, the halls
and chambers of the palace.
What is this signal

that echoes through the poem
and startles me awake
each night at 4?

Tbilisi Thoughts

You must disregard the silence
of the left side
of the poem.

You must disregard the howling
of the right side
of the poem,

the child soldiers at the city gates
with orphaned poems
on their bayonets.

Pay no heed
to the rats in the granary
or the thieves

who would steal the morning light
from the poem,
the lamplight from the poem,

the inner light from the poem,
the darkness of the poem
from the poem.

You must disregard
the sex of the poem
if you can,

if you can.
Never tell the poem
what is to be done.

Never beg for mercy
from the poem,
since it can offer none.

Do not ask
what language it speaks,
since the answer is none.

Remember that the light and the dark
are the same,
if you can,

if you can,
that the I
and the Thou are the same,

the above and the below,
the far and the near.
Embrace the words you cannot hear.

A Tiny Cup

My dying
friend,
offered a tiny
cup
of vodka,
sips
it
so gingerly

We

It has been declared that
we
have two national sports,
football and war.
The profits from one
are even greater
than those from the other.
It is up to
you
to decide which.

Take 1

The singers and their heroin.
Oval-mouthed, she floats above him,
then he over her and then
the song, the song,
and then the warmth, the rush, the plunge,
and then they float alone.

There is a power, a powder,
within the song
that lasts forever
and never lasts for long.
One minute young, next minute gone.
So the singers, so the song.

Eyes Listening

Your resemblance to the Angel of Death
is uncanny, as is that of the catalpa
now briefly flowering once again
here by the Avenida of Counterfeit Songs
where language at last reaches its end.

Still we continue, oceans apart,
breath upon breath, our thoughts in our arms,
even as the torchlight parades
return so avidly to fashion. It's true
I once failed to return your glance

and our futures changed,
almost imperceptibly at first,
each lost in the maze-like streets
of different cities not
of our choosing, I among my tattered

maps, you in endlessly evolving thrall
to the hive and the web and the fearsome
psalm of all the hours to come
in the haphazard course of this turning world
where words hurled

through the air
could not save us.

The Writing of the Poem

The writing of the poem
and the suicide of the silent singer
must have occurred

at roughly the same time.
Ranky Tanky was playing. I
don't recall the song—

maybe the one
about how life goes on
until it's gone—

maybe another.
The prayer beads fell
from my hand once again.

They were fashioned from some ancient
and pitted wood that must have darkened
over time I'm told.

Her voice seemed to be enclosed within,
her words dark and clear,
or did I simply imagine them there?

The poem itself was terrible of course,
since it had no beginning or end.
Often I drop things now.

To Sister

And then a thing called thought,
a swift in the air
until caught

Pillows of Stone

A man is talking to a wall
A woman is weeping by a well

We ask the words to do their work
but they have nothing to tell

The ancient mulberry is finally dying
The tales it's heard will vanish as well

Perhaps it will yet outlast me
Impossible to tell

I imagine them gathering elsewhere,
these friends so recently gone

So as one we'll chant *Down With Love*
and rest our heads on pillows of stone

We've sung all of this before of course
but still it remains unknown—

the woman, the well, the man at the wall,
the endless talk and the pillars of stone

One more drink to the swollen moon then,
whose face has nothing to tell

T(here)

There we were in The Dreamers Café
having seen our dreams erased.

I was drinking bitter tea.
Outside a nameless river flowed.

We could have been anywhere,
might have been anywhere,

might be anywhere,
chanted my companion in this life.

How would we know?
We must amuse ourselves

with the tea of irony, the tea
of despair, here

among the scattered tables,
here among the half-assed jokes

in tongues we cannot understand.
We laugh anyway

in order not to understand
as they dance on tabletops,

these beautiful children
nameless as the river.

And if it is sleep
that offers such a poem

so be it
as night turns into day.

(St. Petersburg, Fontanka, 2015)

Far Shore

The book was called Bone,
then Blood, finally Dust, red
dust which settled all around us.

So we'll to the woods no more.
We'll hew close to the shore
despite the coming storm.

And we'll abandon the ill-lit corridors
with their plethora of signs
and the names on every door.

And we'll study the signs no more
for what beneath may lie.
The book was called Desire after all,

though not made of words exactly,
something closer to the cries and roars
you heard at the big top circus

as a child, a child both lost
and found, like bodies along a shore
("sign of our times" she'd said),

she the lost lover in a print dress,
a worn print dress,
unconcerned by death,

unchanged by death.
I remember her swimming
back and forth along that shore,

heedless of wave and tide,
neck and shoulders glistening,
where other bodies now dot the shore.

"Death has become regrettably commonplace,"
noted a friend, a hologram
in Prague,

who proceeded to dance a final dance,
and then another,
a water dance.

But the poem
can say nothing of that,
nothing of what is music

and what is not,
nothing of the words we borrow
from cliff-heads and scudding clouds,

from the dust itself
and the madman's glance,
or from the upturned, open

mouths of singers, the singers
beyond themselves and song,
so we'll to the woods once more.

Since You Asked

Yes, it's true, that snow
is often likened to poetry, slant
winds are likened to poetry,
sickle moons, violent crime—only

the most violent of crimes—as well.
Music is absolved of poetry,
war in love with poetry.
(All war thinks it's poetry.)

The ministers of Birkenau
recited poetry
to their wee bairns at night,
curled in their beds

like lullabies
and preparing to dream
of snow and more snow.
The Caesars sowed blood

wherever they showed up
and called it poetry.
The executioner's song
is a form of poetry,

one that will outlast poetry,
for so it is sung.
The tides of the Thames
cough up ancient coins,

condoms, daggers and clay pipes,
but never poetry,
because such things are poetry itself.
And those sharpened spikes

tipped with curare
exist on the spines of books
to protect you from poetry
since you asked.

But since you did ask,
there is no protection
from poetry,
not even this.

MIDNIGHTS

"It was then that I embarked on my investigations. I wasn't short of material: rather the excess of it drove me to distraction in my dark hours."

Kafka, *Investigations of a Dog*

Midnights: Thinking now

Thinking now
near midnight
of Beckett
years back
late evening
at the Closerie
des Lilas
saying—sotto
voce—All
I'm searching for
is *word*, not
the word, not
a word,
just *word*.

(As re-
   counted to
me, likewise
   near midnight,
and likewise
   many years
back, by
   Bob Creeley.)

Midnights: La jetée

Will the fires yes the
fires will consume us.

We will scatter our own
ashes, scatter them in a spiral

between lake and sky,
cadmium yellow sky.

The lovers, intertwined,
will speak of this

at lakeside, will say nothing
of this by water's edge.

They will taste the salt
on each other's lips

and discover the pain
of the salt light,

salt where the sculptor
once signaled with his hands

a little to the left,
a little to the right,

amid the tides.
Is it he or I

who would say,
Out of salt we are made?

Only a fool
like myself

would write of this
at midnight

among the fires
when all

should be left
in silence.

Midnights: As midnight approached

As midnight approached I asked
her to send me a word.

What is a word?
was her reply.

What is midnight, she asked,
and where and when

and why?

Midnights: Outside

Sometime
after midnight
Han Shan

came down
once again
from the mountain.

Do you realize
we have no tongue
in common?

he asked,
innocently
enough.

So how is it
we are speaking
one with another

or is it no
one to no one—
across the countless

dynasties, the infinite
revolutions of the spheres
and twilight murmurations—

speaking about
that rag-and-bone
shop most foul

of the heart's slowing clock?
About the hangman's knot?
Speaking about

the breath-turn, the pause,
about desire, about loss?
In my time, remember,

the empty universe
was permitted,
had its honored place,

and stillness
was the celebrated dance.
In my time, remember,

there were no
midnights, no streetlights,
no zoetropes or pantographs,

no April in Paris, no
suicides
in room 309.

So let us go then,
you and I, to
that place where

there is no time.
What were names
after all, when

I was alive,
when you and
I were alive?

Who was Cold Mountain
after all, who
our blessed company,

Last Wolf and Lost Wolf
howling at the Drinking Gourd,
and who that friend Villon

in tattered cloak
amidst the snows?
So let us go

then, nameless,
you and I,
and find our way outside.

Midnights: So Han Shan

Turn out the lights
so you can see
what's happening.

So Han Shan,
his advice,
'round midnight.

Midnights: Strange Speech

What am I to think
of that friend, half mad,
addicted to strange speech?

What am I to think
of his thought,
the butterflies and galaxies,

the circling stars,
the seas
that rise

each hour
up to his eyes
only to recede?

What am I to think
of his prayers
to the Unwanted Gods,

gods with no followers,
the homeless gods
forever wandering

beyond the walled garden?
What am I to think
of the pillars of fire

he's willingly embraced
or of his name
which changes by the day?

A forlorn fiddle
lies at his feet,
martyr to midnight's song.

Oh fiddle, oh friend
let us never forget
to play the notes wrong.

Midnights: Alberto Caeiro you

Alberto Caeiro you,
having neither lived nor died,
nor having written one
word of your collected works,
are free in a way
none of the rest
of us can claim,
we whose poems
melt in our paws, we
who whine
about the dying of the light
even as we whisper
our praises to midnight,
its silences and chimes,
midnight at once
both beginning and end,
while you sing those fields,
those vague fields, bare trees,
invisible before your eyes,
sing too the cries
of water birds unheard,
you who have never
been battered by storm
or blinded by the sun,
and having never known
the body of another
or the jagged path of thought,
you, no more than a name,
yet alone among us real,
like such stars as are flowers.

Midnights: A lifetime

It took me a lifetime
of midnights
to realize
that signifier and signified
are just a bunch of jive.

Midnights: Alberto Caeiro

Because whoever loves never knows what he loves
Nor why he loves, nor what it means to love ...
                    —Alberto Caeiro

It is a wonder
late at night
to open at last
The Complete Works
of Alberto Caeiro
(whom I once knew
quite well),
a man who
so to speak
did not exist
and whose maker
(whom I knew
quite well
as well)
also, like most of us,
did not so
to speak exist.
The world
has fallen apart
many times, Alberto,
since you uncomposed
these poems, yet
through it all
you have neither
lived nor died,
while the sunflower
and the butterfly
escaped the poem
among those invisible
lightning fields
where you thrived.

Midnights: The Unnamable

So it is written that on the Sabbath the Unnamable One, Blessed be His Name, voided a perfect, soft and odorless turd. So pleased was He with His creation that He named it after Donald, the Trumpff, Blessed be His Name.

And so it came to pass that in the decades following, a Festival of the Trumpff Turd took place each year around the globe, until rising seas and engulfing fires covered the lands and extinguished all life, a tad sooner than anticipated.

Midnights: The wind

The wind
is blowing clouds
across the moon

once again.
At least
there is truth

to this
though I can offer
no proof.

Midnights: Is there no end

Is there no end
to the drawings we make
of ourselves making drawings

of ourselves making drawings
of ourselves, no end
to the tales we tell

of our multiple selves, our
sundered selves, invisible selves?
No end to the words

telling of other words
searching for other worlds, forgotten
worlds, parallel worlds,

worlds of labyrinth, flight
and fall, fractured odes,
torch-lit halls? No end

to the drawings we erase
as the light fades,
or to the renga chains

we cast aside
incomplete?
No end

of midnights
until the last wolf
with searing eyes

has sung the last poem
and the last poem
has sounded its last alarm?

Midnights: As I approach . . .

Near midnight, as I approach Saturn (this so-called "failed sun"), and the myriad intricacies of its icy rings become clearer and clearer, the realization that my own end is quite near grows stronger and comes, like the rings, into ever-sharpening focus.

So be it.

We are told that space ("outer space") is silent, but this is wrong. Traveling through it we hear the music of the spheres, echoes like agonized cries and infinite, discrete whispers, congregating as if across time, or precisely across time.

Music for compline?

As to time: I was raised through my childhood years in a cave high above ground. That cave had a name, and that name was a number, but I will address that at another time.

Or not.

I adapted to the name as best I could, before escape, but not without pain.

There was everywhere in that cave a thin film of ice that seemed to me then like a portrait of time.

And the voyage: Titan, its methane seas, Rhea, Dione,

Pan, Atlas, Enceladus.

How many more such Saturnian moons, in passing, might I name,

and how many ghost ships to greet me, or greet us, on those chemical waves?

Or not.

And my end, as above, still not precisely known as far as I can tell, or is it already inscribed on some page I have not as yet read?

So be it.

Midnights: Corona: Personae

At last
we wear our masks
in the open

So laughs
Han
Shan

Midnights: Caucasus

Midnight, and my gaze falls upon a sheaf of translations of my work into a language outside my comprehension. What makes the Georgian script so beautiful (if impenetrable) to my eye? Is it simply the association with enduring memories of sudden, brisk breezes, early strawberries and dark mountain honey, along with company both specific and various, soft voices by a roadside in the Caucasus? Is it the tragic historical memory such a script enfolds? Or is it the impenetrability itself, as such, or beauty solely in itself, as such, and its untranslatability?

(Please tell me if you know, Nuka, and even if you don't.)

Midnights: Words

Words only get in the way

so they say

Midnights: Vico

Giambattista, for all
our shared flaws
of mind and heart
in this spinning world
do we not
together understand
that there is
but one midnight
that endlessly recurs?
Always same always different.

Midnights: Corona Song

So night

was a dark bloom that grew

steadily,

steadily darker and wider.

It muffled our sounds,

our whispers and cries.

The exit signs

led us in circles

for countless dark hours

until we reached the one

that said No Exit.

Did we believe it?

Do we believe it still?

Did we lie still

in that dark bloom

that muffled all sound

whether soft or shrill,

all those rippling notes

rising from the sleeper's throat:

the singer's taut throat,

the lover's silken throat?

Did we believe the summer snows

when they suddenly came,

and then the winter footsteps

left by night in them?

Believe that time's

dark bloom, dark

wound, would

keep its muffled word

in a translated world

ministered by chance,

the thing as it is,

both quiet and loud?

Will we find our way out?

Midnights: COBRA: Amsterdam

The artists of the COBRA group, all long dead, visited me and tore at my flesh for having insulted their collective aesthetic catastrophes. Can you not understand a compliment, I asked, even when offered innocently in a dream? Can you not see your paintings and drawings arrayed on the walls of my dream, as I sleep uneasily in a hotel by the Herengracht? Can you not let me drink my sleep in peace, while all-too-familiar ghosts roam the halls and bodies pile up in the canal? Can you not at least listen when I cry out among the angelic orders, as midnight takes hold of its brush and configures the darkness that is ours?

Midnights: Kathleen (Far Away Near)

Old Angel Midnight
appeared to me
as I attempted to visit

the Village of Hermes.
Those gates are closed
to you, said he,

didn't you know,
until you discover the key,
and for that you must ask

Kathleen, Kathleen
who will tell you
that there is

no key, Kathleen
who will tell you
to move and so to see,

to move and so to speak
of a signal
that has gone out,

the burning of the palace,
the fragmentation of tongues
and the fire beneath the ground,

so The Gate of Desire,
The Gate of Breath,
The Gate of Birds,

and so Kathleen who
will tell you, that there
is, never was, a key.

The Chimes at Midnight

King Ubu is moping on his throne.

He pines for his golf, but the weather is bad.

Many tens of thousands of his subjects are dying, even though he ordered them not to.

He commanded them not to.

He remembers that early on he commanded them not to.

Very early on.

They have disobeyed him.

His hair of spun gold is getting itchy.

That turd he stashed in his tunic seems to be heating up.

He feels lonely and needs some pussy but doesn't know where to reach.

For it.

He has already achieved perfection in his governance, so he knows not what more there is to attain.

Perhaps another meal of souls will quell his pain.

Moloka'i Midnights

The directive came down from King Ubu himself, signed with his characteristic, slightly smudged, X. Those subjects identifiable as poets were to be selected and transported to Moloka'i to replace the now aged and rapidly diminishing colony of lepers concentrated there. Like the lepers preceding them, the poets were to be officially designated as "legally dead." King Ubu, it goes without saying, had never actually read any poetry, though he had occasionally heard, or rather overheard, it during his increasingly rare forays among the populace. At least he'd assumed it was poetry, since it sounded odd and made no sense. In short, it gave offense. And clearly it was not edible, which to the perennially famished Ubu, the eternally unsated Ubu, was of paramount consideration. "Poetic licentiousness" was the legal rationale for the order of resettlement. And so these wordsmiths (mysteriously, some capitalized, others not)—vanguardists, neo-classicists, conceptualists, concretists, Futurists, metametaphorists, absurdists, Negritude poets, slam poets, New Formalists, Fugitives, Agrarians, Nuyoricans, New York School, Beats, Symbolists, Dadaists, Spoken Word, Oulipians, Confessionals, establishment minions—no matter—were removed from their cold-water flats, their fifth floor walkups, their garrets, their industrial lofts, their fetid and ill-illuminated university offices, their pastoral studios, their *chambres de bonne*, and forcibly transported to the island paradise to which they had been consigned.

THANK YOU, UBU!

Midnights: Sugar

Late one night I opened a book
by a much-lauded English
author of novels and short fiction.

She appeared to me and said,
Put that down, Sugar,
you don't give

even the tiniest shit
about stories,
and you know it.

May Day Midnight

In the light of day
perhaps all of this
will make sense.

But have we come this far,
come this close to death,
just to make sense?

Midnights: Godard/Lamarr

I told myself there were no more real
poems left to write, only fake poems,

which were after all the best,
like fake snow in a ballet,

as silent as a pirouette
or a wind-blown flag planted on the moon,

silent as the ghost in the machine
or the ghost of Godard in a machine

or a fog machine in something noir
or the ghost of Hedy Lamarr

seeking refuge from a film by Godard,
a silent film by Godard,

in which the only thing to be heard
is the voice of Hedy Lamarr,

the bitter-sweet accent of Hedy Lamarr,
speaking words that can't be heard or seen,

words known only to Hedy Lamarr
and only fully known very late,

near the silent midnight
of an unknowable life.

Question: Midnight

Late one night
a dear philosopher friend

ageing like me
leaned over and asked,

Is *This Thing*
worse for you

or for me?
Yes, I replied, definitely.

Midnights: Blue

My first suicide, not designed by me exactly, was to take up poetry. My second, not designed by me exactly, was to write the poem "Sun" over the course of a year. Each was performed with ink ("Midnight Blue"), and each, like all suicides, represented at once a kind of opening and a kind of closure, an orderly sequence of midnights bathed in clarifying light, free of flamboyant gesture or operatic excess. Then the third, both far away and near. You will have foreseen it, if you understand me as well as I (do not) understand myself, as well as I (do not) foresee the words to come, the midnights like stanzas, the tales to be unspooled as such time arrives, as if any of us have ever known time "to arrive."

The third as I watched a heron near a muddy pond—not midnight, not yet, not quite.

After Midnight

Sometime after midnight
Han Shan drifted down
a mountain path
and arrived in my dream
only to announce
that every angel is terrifying,
also that heron you saw
by the muddy pond
was not real.

You, reader,
may believe this or not.
Han Shan said
that he does not
though he spoke
such words
to me
as if
they were his own.

Midnights: Crazy Han Shan

Crazy Han
Shan put

finger to
lips

and said,
If you

can't improve
upon

the silence
of deep night,

then please
just shut

the fuck
up.

Midnights: Cranky Han Shan

Cranky Han Shan
stood before the glow
of Rothko's

Number 14
on the bleached wall
of a hushed

white cube.
Why the fuck,
for so he remarked,

is this here
and not out somewhere
in the mountain air?

Midnights: Wise Han Shan

As I scribble
these "Midnights"
in the dark,
wise Han
Shan advises,
Above all,
don't get them right!

Midnights: Moments

Were all our "inadmissible dreams" to be realized, our fractured life-dance would end even more jaggedly.

So it is that we spend our moments or midnights fashioning a language from that which cannot be said.

Tattered fabric of that single sentence Bergson tells us we weave across a lifetime? Pauses, commas, turns of breath, but no periods until that final, full stop?